7 GOLD STANDARDS OF FACILITY CONSTRUCTION

Save Money on Your Next Facilities Construction Project

I0161454

There are many ways to provide construction services for facilities. The GOLD Standard Facility Contractor provides Value-Added Services that help the owner or facility manager to plan the project effectively from the beginning to the end, and at the same time and money.

by

Tom Pritscher, LEED® AP, FMP

with

Ronald A. McKenzie, NCARB

Published by D.E.M. Publishing
A Division of COMPASS Consultants Corporation

i

7 GOLD STANDARDS OF FACILITY CONSTRUCTION
Save Money on Your Next Facilities Construction Project

by

Tom Pritscher, LEED® AP, FMP

All Rights Reserved

Copyright © 2019

Published by D.E.M. Publishing,
A Division of COMPASS Consultants Corporation
"A Competitive Advantage Company"
For information, please contact: ramckenzie.compass@gmail.com
ISBN: 978-1-7339-3200-4
10 9 8 7 6 5 4 3 2 1
First Edition

UNDERSTANDING of LIMIT OF LIABILITY/ DISCLAIMER AND WARRANTY

7 GOLD STANDARDS OF FACILITY CONSTRUCTION
Save Money on Your Next Facilities Construction Project

Table of Contents

Table of Contents

Dedication

*"**THIS BOOK IS DEDICATED TO MY MOTHER,** Suzanne Pritscher, whose consistent love and encouragement have made all the difference. Throughout my life, as a young boy to as recently as yesterday, she has made me feel like I can do anything. With that confidence in hand, I have lived a meaningful life and built a company that has positively impacted its employees and clients. I owe it all to her and am forever grateful."*

Tom Pritscher

The Gold Standard

ORIGINALLY, A GOLD STANDARD referred to gold being the official measure of money. Now, the expression GOLD STANDARD is used to convey VALUE.

As an example, Olympians are the GOLD STANDARD for athletes, or a gold standard is considered the best of the best.

Definition: GOLD STANDARD

1. A monetary standard under which the basic unit of currency is defined by a stated quantity of gold.

2. A paragon of excellence.

   A. Academic education is the gold standard against which other educational activities are judged.

   B. An ideal instance; a perfect embodiment of a concept.

Definition and examples of ''Gold Standard' from vocabulary.com and other on-line sources.

Foreward

FACILITY CONSTRUCTION HAS CHANGED. As you will learn in the following pages, the processes used by many engineering companies are starting to be employed in the construction environment. For a company to provide GOLD Standard Facility Construction Services, they must develop exceptional management ideas with the highest standards, and then implement them across all levels of the business, separating their business from your competitors. As we shall see, the process of reducing management oversight increases the quality of the work at a lower cost to the owners.

Consider the following scenario; a construction company may claim to have four project managers, but what they really have are four different construction companies within the same business! The reason is, each project manager comes to the business with a different background, and hence, they have "their way" of managing the project. The weakness here is this company has failed to recognize the value of developing a GOLD Standard since different project managers run the project their way. So, suddenly there are multiple forms and checklists, different procedures and paperwork for bidding, different managing styles for the on-site superintendent resulting in cost increases for doing business, and in the end, the client loses.

Fortunately, the use of systems methodologies developed around a GOLD Standard has a proven history of increasing performance. There are many ways to provide GOLD Standard Services:

- Provide value-added services,

- Develop internal processes and methodologies so that implementation is uniform throughout the company,

- Develop system checks and balances to continually improve,

- Hire the best people, and,

- Provide in-house training programs to provide continuity of services.

When the best processes are used, the result is the ability to provide a better service for clients. Also, there is the advantage that other project managers can step in and do someone else's job, meaning there are backup plans in place to ensure a smooth flow of work.

Developing a GOLD Standard requires leadership and commitment to "processes" that exceed all expectations. For example, as mentioned before, having the very best people on staff with capability and experience and then developing training programs so all follow the same project methodologies is a huge benefit to a client on multiple levels. It increases the quality of the work and reduces the construction schedule which lowers the project cost to the customer.

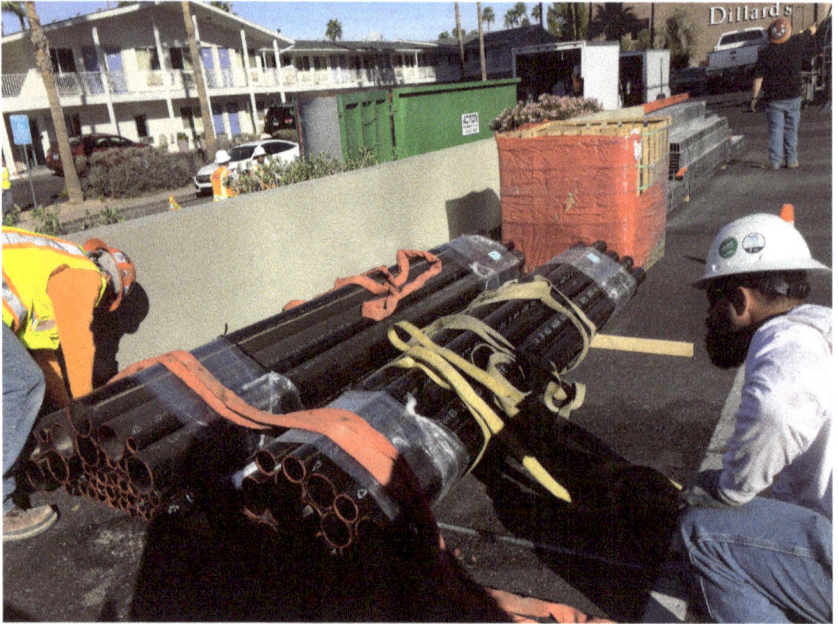

Understanding the GOLD Standard of Facility Construction provides a basis for learning the substance of what the GOLD Standard is all about; the result is the value provided which will be hard to match. For example, how many times does a project manager near the end of construction and the on-site superintendent (or roving superintendent) is pulled off to start a new project, resulting in an unfinished punch list and delayed occupancy. Why does this happen?

The reason is that particular contractor is interested in ramping up the next project thereby capturing a future revenue stream. Meanwhile, the existing project suffers as others step in to complete the work. Here is the difference:

The GOLD Standard Facility Contractor understands that providing the very best service to their clients, is in itself, the very best source of new work. Abandoning the punch list along with the inconvenience of delays to that client will, for the most part, impact future work and referrals.

Also, a company that uses a GOLD Standard as a benchmark will have in place a methodology to seamlessly complete the punch list easily and quickly. That's the difference between a GOLD Standard and just a bid-and-build contractor.

INTRODUCTION: 7 VALUE-ADDED SECRETS

THE GOLD STANDARD OF FACILITY CONSTRUCTION is an important concept, as it means the facility services provided go beyond what is typical of the industry. The GOLD Standard looks at the REAL VALUE that can help the owner with their facility and develops internal processes to provide that value quickly and easily.

The GOLD Standard is developed by asking the question: What does the building owner want when it comes to hiring facility construction services?

7 Gold Standards of Facility Construction

1. Contractor Selection — Contractor Selection discusses the key points of construction delivery as well as their differences. It will help an owner and a facility manager understand the different ways a project can be delivered.

2. Full-Service General Contractor — The advantages of a Full-Service General Contractor is explained and the benefits of the Open Book process and Single Source Responsibility.

3. Pre-Construction Services — The value of pre-construction services means that the owner is going to save money and occupy the project sooner.

4. Working in the Occupied Environment — Working in the occupied environment allows the business to continue to serve their customers, which is a tremendous advantage to the owner. The talents of an experienced facility contractor who can envision the entire project and all the separate stages of construction.

5. Safety Plans — Safety is the most important issue in construction. But there's a big difference between many of the safety plans that contractors use if something unexpected happens.

6. Information Transfer — When the project ends, there is a specific process to bring the owner's facility manager up to speed on the systems of the building. This transfer of information is critical to the building's use for future maintenance of the built environment. Compare this to the contractors that quickly move on to the next job delaying the punch list and information transfer.

7. A New Way to Manage — The Value of Partnering.

Chapter One
Contractor Selection

SOONER OR LATER, AN OWNER OF A FACILITY or the facility manager, must hire a contractor or sub-contractor to maintain, upgrade or expand their facility. There are many considerations, such as price, quality, Open Book and schedule. So, the first question is, who do I trust and believe will provide the best service? The following are important considerations:

A. Whom Should I Hire and Why?
B. How are Construction Services Delivered?
C. Broker Contractor vs. Full-Service Contractor
D. Superintendents Assigned to More than One Job
E. Account Manager and Working Foreman
F. Low Bidder is Not Always the Best

A. WHOM SHOULD I HIRE AND WHY?

The answer is both straightforward and complicated. The owner should hire a capable and experienced contractor that fits the project and delivers the most value. The hard part is figuring out which company is the right fit at the right price. There are several parameters to look at when addressing this question. A starting point is to understand how services are delivered.

B. HOW ARE CONSTRUCTION SERVICES DELIVERED?

The advantages and disadvantages of the different construction delivery systems must be compared and are critical to the overall success of any project regarding expectations.

The four delivery methods are as follows:

Design-Bid-Build — An architect designs the project based on a budget and the owner's needs and wants, and prepares schematic drawings, and then later contract documents consisting of construction drawings and specifications. Next is the selection of the general contractor, generally based upon a lump sum price. The lowest qualified bidder is usually selected and is awarded the project. The architect observes the construction and provides administration of the contracts. These are usually "closed book" meaning the owner does not know the price of the subcontracts.

What is known as hard-bid and is recommended by many, including attorneys, as the only way that the lowest possible price can be obtained as there is competitive bidding. This is not necessarily true, because there are competitive bids, or should be, in other delivery methods as well.

In the Design-Bid-Build delivery method, there can be adversarial relationships developed between the three main participants: the architect, contractor and the owner. Finger pointing usually is the result of a contractor creating issues with the architect in regards to the drawings or specifications to get more money. This situation can also occur at the subcontractor level. It happens quite often and is why the low price is sometimes not the best price. A contractor may elect to submit a low price to capture the project, and start a series of change orders requesting more time and money. As we shall see, a team approach combined with an "OPEN BOOK" is a better approach.

- **Design/Build** — Design and Construction Services are packaged under one contract, or group of contracts, as a single source of project delivery for all design and construction services. There are many variations of this service depending upon who the design-builder is (architect, contractor or engineer) and whether it's in-house or all under one company.

The main difference is Design/Build avoids the adversarial relationships that often occur in the Design-Bid-Build delivery scenario. Design/Build is a team approach usually with a fixed fee and a guaranteed maximum price (GMP), based upon a specified scope of work. Like most delivery systems, if the scope changes, so does the fee.

Usually, a Request for Qualifications (RFQ), or Request for Proposal (RFP), or similar document, are issued by the owner or their representative, and after reviewing the proposals, several are selected for interviews. Based upon that, the contract is awarded.

Because this is a team approach, the price is determined relatively early on in the project, and value engineering occurs along with project scheduling. Very often they will "fast-track" the project, meaning they will start the site work as soon as the foundations are designed and approved by the local building department that has jurisdiction. As the work begins, the final architectural drawings are completed while the construction moves forward, saving time and allowing for a faster occupancy.

Many people will say there are no check and balances in Design/Build as everyone is on the same team. As a team develops the project together, there are check and balances, and there is competitive bidding of the sub-contractors.

- **Construction Management** — A Construction Manager (CM) acts as an agent of the owner, and manages the entire process, from hiring the architect, to all the subs, and coordinates the schedules and budgets for a fixed fee. The main benefit of this delivery method is the sub-contracts are still competitively bid, but there is no markup on the price to the owner. CM companies market their services to prospects in advance of hiring the architect, allowing them to capture the project early by becoming an agent of the owner.

- **Performance Contracting** — Another construction delivery method is known as Performance Contracting and is relatively new. This delivery method is based on an energy audit, and the proposal for construction work is made based on saving energy. The energy savings are passed on to the Performance Contractor, who funded the project, as payment for services. Performance Contracting may be part of a facilities contractor delivery option as part of a larger project.

- Maybe adding other newer delivery systems, mainly Integrated Project Delivery (IPD).

The above delivery systems are used throughout the industry on a wide range of projects, large and small, including facility build-outs, maintenance, and roofing projects. Most of these contractors are classified as broker contractors who sub out most of the work, particularly the most important, the drywall, paint and interior finishes.

However, a GOLD Standard Facility Contractor approaches the project from a different perspective. They listen to the owner needs and wants and submit a plan that responds to these requirements. Keeping in mind the most effective way of delivering the services that helps the owner. Nevertheless, it's important to understand the overall delivery options.

C. BROKER CONTRACTOR VS. FULL-SERVICE CONTRACTOR

A <u>Broker Contractor</u> is a company that bids all work out to a variety of subs and management companies that outsource project managers and superintendents.

On the other hand, a Full-Service Contractor performs all of the work – they are a

Single Source of Responsibility taking a "hands-on" approach for the entire project. The project is staffed with their employees wearing company shirts. No longer are there strangers walking around the construction site.

D. SUPERINTENDENTS ASSIGNED TO MORE THAN ONE JOB

A client visits the job site of his new project, and when there is no personnel on the job site or in the construction trailer, they start to wander around, and finally find someone.

"Where is the superintendent?" the client asks.

Eventually, the client finds out that the superintendent runs two other projects, and hops around from job site to job site. While a standard practice with a lot of construction companies, to save money, it does open the door for potential problems, and even accidents and safety issues. What if there is a major decision that affects the construction activities and the overall schedule? Or, a question comes up regarding the painting spec or hundreds of other situations that need a response from the superintendent?

What happens is the sub simply makes their own decision because "time-is-money." Sometimes these decisions turn out for the worse costing the contractor money. As always, the contractor will try to recoup that money leading to change orders.

As we shall see, supervision of the construction project is important because the consequences of not supervising the construction can immensely impact many parts of the project including final project closeout and customer satisfaction. All kinds of BAD things can happen when there is not true supervision on a project, such as:

- The project can be laid out improperly creating a whole host of expensive problems.

- The timing of the completion of the project can be impacted because different trades were not sequenced correctly.

- The trades are not supervised creating compatibility problems between materials.

- Materials are substituted without prior knowledge creating issues relating to the scope of work.

- Formal inspections of the construction by the municipalities fail, creating costly delays and possible demolition or other expensive activities to bring the Work into compliance.

The list goes on. There is no question that on-site supervision is an important part of the construction process. Supervision itself is a tangible activity, but what is important is the intangible consequences of how a project is supervised. Here are some guidelines:

- The superintendent should be on-site, focused on one job and not running two or three different projects at any given time.

- The superintendents should be trained by authoritative organizations such as the Associated General Contractors of America (AGC), and the Associated Builders and Contractors (ABC), so they know and understand the responsibilities and consequences of how they can affect the outcome of a project.

- The background of a superintendent should include being a journeyman carpenter. With this training, the superintendent will know exactly how a project will come together, as well as how different materials relate to each other.

- Superintendents should be leaders.

These guidelines help the owner get the project result they want and desire; it helps the facility manager in their day-to-day facilities role.

From the owners' and subcontractors' point-of-view, supervision helps to have a smooth running and well-managed site. Top-notch supervision means the general contractor has a commitment to quality and is focused on the customer. **Good supervision is a commitment that starts at the top.**

"One of the advantages of a GOLD Standard Facility Contractor is they always use an on-site superintendent. Many construction companies use a project manager or a superintendent who checks in on the job every couple of days. From the owners and subcontractors point-of-view, on-site supervision helps to have a smooth running and well-managed site and reflects a high level of commitment to quality and focus on the customer."

Jody Hawkins, LEED Green Associate, CFM, SFP – Facility Manager, Best Western International, Inc

One important step an owner and a facility manager can take is to meet the superintendent that will be assigned the project before construction starts during the interview process. The superintendent is the one person that will be on the job full-time, and their role should start as early as possible, even during the preliminary award phase, before they start to conduct the project.

E. ACCOUNT MANAGER AND WORKING FOREMAN

A GOLD Standard Facility Contractor has an Account Manager assigned to a project that works with a full-time, (never leaving the job site) Working Foreman.

Construction is the art of coordination. How can you coordinate if there's no one there to coordinate with when you need them? Everyone certainly understands that all businesses are looking for ways to cut expenses, and by having part-time superintendents is one way to do that. However, A GOLD Standard Facility Contractor looks at the big picture and realizes it's cost effective in a long run to provide a high level of service that includes permanent full-time Working Foreman on the job site, as well as using all their own employees to build the project.

F. LOW BIDDER IS NOT ALWAYS THE BEST

Price is subjective as one bidder may include a service, such as street cleaning, while the other one doesn't. Or, many times, particularly in hard bid situations, what appears to be the low price is actually the price with the biggest mistake. Some attorneys have advised that it's the bidder's fault and encourage an owner to accept the price as a sign of good fortune. But going into a project knowing the bidder is going to lose money only leads to a nightmare construction project where the quality and timeline will be impacted. By the time you figure that out, it's too late. That's the reason why it's important to understand how services are delivered.

It's important to understand that some companies use an artificially low price as their strategy.

What this means is they may know what the right price is but that's their little secret. A contractor does their take-off but looks for areas of debate that can lead to a change-order for money and/or time. They're seeking to capture the project with a low bid and then as the project moves through the different phases, issue change orders to get to their desired profit level, or even more depending upon how experienced their client is in purchasing construction services.

"One of the biggest advantages of a GOLD Standard Facility Contractor is they are honest, open and transparent right from the beginning of the project in terms of project cost. Many construction companies bid low to win the job and later rely on change orders creating a false cost expectation for the owner. With GOLD Standard Facility Contractor there is a peace of mind that the contractor is working in the best interest of the owner and has included all of the scope in the original cost."

Dhaval Gajjar, Ph. D., FMP, SFP, Clemson University

Not having the correct price harms the client in numerous ways. They may spend their funds on another project, and then when more money is requested they run into problems. Having the right price means that the customer can plan much better and make better financial decisions.

Contractor Selection

GOLD STANDARD

The facility manager, or building owner's biggest question, is what contractor they should hire? What's a good fit for one owner may not be a good fit for another. As an owner, you will interview different contractors as part of the selection process. Ask yourself this question: Do they listen to me? The contractor that listens to your concerns is without question the one you want to hire, because they are going to provide a much better response to your needs and wants. For example, you're in a meeting and if a contractor's cell phone rings (it shouldn't by the way), and they pull it out of their pocket to see who it is, or worse yet, answer it, then you know that's not the contractor for you.

Chapter Two
Full-Service General Contractor

LET'S FACE IT, CONSTRUCTION COSTS are going up, and it's becoming more-and-more expensive to build. Increased construction costs are the result of multiple factors impacting different areas of the construction process. If it's not a rise in the price of steel, then it's a change in the cost of concrete or renegotiated labor contracts. The list is endless.

It's important to understand that the GOLD Standard Facility Full Service Contractor uses an OPEN BOOK process, meaning that the client sees all the contracts, and knows exactly how their money is spent. The Open Book Process is discussed below and is an important point in understanding Facility Construction.

A. Cost Plus

B. Open Book

C. Exploring Project Expectations

D. Self-Performing - Sole Source Responsibility

A. COST PLUS

In private work, when selecting a contractor, a great approach is to assemble the best team at the onset or as the project develops. Some might refer to this as a partnering approach. A team works together for the benefit of the owner; this way, everyone wins. Without question, a project will cost a specific sum of money, and it's the responsibility of the contractor to manage the budget, but this sum is unknown at the beginning of the project.

For example, say a project is estimated to cost $1 million. First, not all contractors have the same management skills, human resource pools or relationships with subcontractors, vendors, and suppliers, not to mention capitalization. Second, there are many unknowns over the course of a project, such as the impact of weather, hidden soil conditions, etc. Given these variables, the project that is expected to cost $1 million may come in for more, or less, depending upon what happens during any phase of the construction process.

From this perspective, owners assembling a team might consider a Cost-Plus approach. In other words, the owner selects the best-qualified contractor that can assist them and the architect in making the most cost-effective and appropriate decisions. They can then contract with their selected general contractor based on a fixed fee for the work.

B. OPEN BOOK

With an Open Book process where all bids can be reviewed, owners can potentially save a substantial sum of money in the long run while getting a building that better fits their needs. The traditional strategy of selecting the lowest bidder fosters an atmosphere of developing the best legal posture while the project participant looks for ways to maximize their individual profits. When this happens, the owner loses and projects tend to have significant cost overruns. In a team approach, the OWNER'S problem becomes the CONTRACTOR'S problem. A general contractor under the team approach helps to find the best solution for the project, not just for themselves, but all the stakeholders involved.

The Open Book process gives owners a solution to this problem, as well as the best value for every construction dollar spent. The Open Book process coupled with a flat fee means the owner is in a better position to save money on the project.

This process benefits everyone on the team, allowing input in product and subcontractor selection decisions.

> "GOLD Standard Facility Contractors who are familiar with the intricacies of the Open Book process can really offer a value-added service to their clients. Why? Because the Open Book process can insure the owner is getting the best purchasing power for every dollar spent. The Open Book process makes a lot of sense as it allows the contractor to join the construction team early, and take part in the planning process by providing value engineering services. It allows you to competitively and equitably bid subcontractors of your choice insuring quality workmanship and a low cost solution."
>
> Terry L. Prisk, MCR, CFM

Contractors who are experienced in this process have the infrastructure in place to pass on the cost savings benefits to their clients.

Contractors who are familiar with the intricacies of the Open Book process provide this value-added service to their clients. Why? Because the Open Book process ensures the owner is getting the best purchasing power for every dollar spent.

An OPEN BOOK / COST PLUS process makes sense for the owner, architect, and general contractor. One proven method is to utilize a flat fee, whereby all construction and reimbursable expenses are multiplied by a flat fee. By establishing a flat fee, the contractor can contribute in numerous ways to make sure the owner gets the most for their money.

Benefits include:

- A phased construction schedule that will fast-track projects and result in earlier completion time.

- The owner's needs are understood by the team who is responsible for delivering the project.

- Construction feasibility of the design can be evaluated early in the design phase.

- Value engineering is an ongoing process that establishes continuous cost information based upon the most economical design choices that meet the owner's needs.

- A stepped permit process, which can allow construction to start sooner and result in an earlier occupancy.

- As subcontractors and vendors submit their bids, all parties can review them.

The Open Book process enables many parts of the design and construction process to occur simultaneously. For example, by using a stepped work permit process, a permit can be taken out by the general contractor for the demolition of a space. That work can begin while work on the drawings continues and the full building permit is secured later. This process speeds up construction, helps the owner save money and results in an early occupancy because the contractor can be reviewing and updating the cost of the project as design continues. (Early occupancy often translates into increased profits for the owner).

C. EXPLORING PROJECT EXPECTATIONS

With the more traditional but slower bid and build process, owners must wait for the completion of the construction documents before learning the cost of a project. The Open Book process offers a continuous, ongoing method of delivering construction services and provides more timely information for the owner. This process doesn't just save time; it saves money. How often can you say that in construction?

As companies grow, many will be faced with expanding their existing facilities or even building new ones to meet their particular needs. To help oversee this process, they will need to hire the expertise of a general contractor. Some companies rely upon the guidance of an architect to pre-qualify and then select a contractor based solely upon the price; when, in reality, there are many factors to consider beyond just the low price bid.

Today's general contractors enter the building cycle much earlier in the project development stage, bringing with them a wealth of pre-construction services. This expertise benefits both the owner as well as the architect regarding overall project scope and costs.

For example, it is the contractor, not the architect, who is responsible for the purchase of construction materials and who contract with subcontractors, meaning the contractor is in a position to provide real cost information and suggestions for new approaches to the "buildability" of the project during the development phase.

D. SELF-PERFORMING — SOLE SOURCE RESPONSIBILITY

When a contractor self-performs the work, it means that they are the sole source responsibility, which creates an increase in communication between trades at the highest level. There is no longer finger pointing between trades.

A GOLD Standard Facility Contractor who self-performs Carpentry Services, Painting, Plumbing, Full Service Electrical, HVAC Filter Changes, separates them from most contractors. Structural steel, concrete, and several other trades are competitively bid. Since the GOLD Standard Facility Contractor uses an Open Book process, those sub bids are not marked up.

The result is that it allows the value-added services to take on real meaning and have a real impact on the final project. These services such as, sole source responsibility, enhanced communications, value engineering, fast-tracking and budget control have a real impact on the entire project.

A contractor, who provides "value engineering" and "project life cycle cost analysis" as part of their pre-construction services, is in a position to offer alternative products and methods of construction during the conceptual phase of the project, rather than after the finalization of the drawings.

Changes after the completion of drawings can increase the project cost significantly. So, how does an owner choose a GOLD Standard Facility contractor? Owners should take a look at their big picture goals and objectives, and then from that perspective, find out which contractor offers the services that best fit the needs of their project. We all know of instances in which contractor selection has led to adversarial relationships during construction. A lot of this has to do with the ability to predict the cost and to properly manage and bring projects in at that cost. We are not talking about public bid work, where, in most cases, the project must go to the lowest bidder, but private work where the selection can go to the most qualified bidder.

Full-Service General Contractor

GOLD STANDARD

There are contractors, and there are contractors. Almost anyone can be a broker contractor where all the trades are bid to subs, as well as site coordination and supervision to management companies. A GOLD Standard Facility Contractor is the Sole Source of Responsibility for the entire project and self-performs much of the work using management methodologies that allow for accurate and high-quality construction.

Chapter Three
Pre-Construction Services

A SKILLED GOLD STANDARD FACILITY CONTRACTOR who provides pre-construction services is in a position to save their client's money compared to a broker contractor who will outsource everything.

Consider the following points:

A. Pre-Construction Services

B. Cost, Time, Quality

C. Capital Expenditures Budget – Four Year Facility Plan

A. PRE-CONSTRUCTION SERVICES

Pre-construction services are designed to assist in the decision-making process associated with project planning. For example, when the work is facility related (such as working in, or adjacent to, an occupied environment) the contractor can provide a wealth of information regarding site usage, construction sequencing, safety and costs before the work starts. The most important issue relates to cost.

A GOLD Standard Facility Contractor offering pre-construction services can analyze the impact of the budget and project choices (i.e., what is this design going to cost compared to an alternate design? Or, what changes need to be made to meet our budgetary guidelines?). The contractor is the only one with hands-on experience relative to cost. They order material every day, they know the cost of manpower, and they know how long a particular construction activity takes. Contractors are in a position to offer accurate construction estimates.

Pre-construction services provided by a GOLD Standard Facility Contractor compliment the architect's services by helping with cost estimates and construction methodology. The architect is still responsible for the design of the spaces relative to the owner's building program. However, incorporating the use of pre-construction services as part of preliminary planning can, without question, save the owner money.

Consider this Idea:

The only time you can save money on a project is before the con-

struction starts. After construction starts, all you do is spend money.

The time to save money is when the construction documents are being prepared. The best way to evaluate a typical project design from the point-of-view of value engineering is during the design process. An owner is going to have to hire a general contractor sooner or later; it's advantageous to do so at the beginning of a project when the general contractor's construction experience can benefit the project development (and the owner's bottom line). The best part is, that the owner still has the advantage of competitive bidding of subcontractors once the project is ready for bid.

Saving time and money are critical needs for the owner/facility manager, who makes decisions regarding a particular facility based upon the objectives set forth by a company's changing needs. These decisions almost always relate to money (i.e., how do I maximize my construction dollars?). When there are so many complex building issues facing today's facility managers – from mechanical, electrical, structural systems, to the actual construction sequencing and coordination – the timely advice from a contractor is necessary.

The real advantage of pre-construction services is that it helps facility managers to manage from a position of strength. They can develop a team of services that work together to guide a project to the best possible solution based on the given design criteria, budget, and construction methodology. Doubts regarding budget concerns are eliminated, and the focus is on producing a quality project that satisfies the programming objectives.

By developing relationships with GOLD Standard Facility Contractors who offer pre-construction services, owners and facility managers have an indispensable resource for construction decisions.

"GOLD Standard pre-construction services is a way to develop and train team members who work together – guiding them and the project to the best possible solution. This is based on a given design criteria, budget, and construction methodology combined with GOLD Standard processes. Without question, the pre-construction services offered by a GOLD Standard Facility Contractor addresses budget right up front which leads to producing a quality project that satisfies the programming objectives and stakeholders."

Rick Corea –On Semiconductor. Director, Global Facilities. IFMA Fellow

B. COST, TIME, QUALITY

Some contractors will say, you can have cost and time, but it might NOT have the quality. Or another contractor will say, I can get the project done in the timeframe you need and at the quality you want, but it's going to cost you. Basically, they're saying, you can have any two, but not all three.

Why not? A GOLD Standard Facility Contractor looks at the big picture regarding the pre-construction services and figures out how to do it. Consider the following components and how they impact Cost, Time and Quality.

1. Value Engineering — Value Engineering is defined by the National Institute of Building Sciences as the following:

"Value Engineering is a conscious and explicit set of disciplined procedures designed to seek out optimum value for both initial and long-term investment."

One way to understand this is how an architect, engineer and contractor can look at the same project from different perspectives. Why? Because each has a different background of experience. The VALUE of Value engineering is when the team works together to put the very best project together.

2. Scheduling — Construction scheduling is an important part of the process, as the schedule drives the project. A construction project, particularly one that involves the occupied environment, is a continuous flow of different but related construction activities that occur in phases designed to minimize the impact to the occupied environment.

In the occupied environment, the project schedule is referred to as the interior phasing schedule, and is an important pre-construction activity. The biggest problem that a contractor faces when doing interior work is how to separate construction from the corporate work areas. One solution is to set up staging areas which will minimize interruptions to the corporate work. Developing an interior phasing schedule allows a construction project to move through a facility in a sequence of planned events. For example, when remodeling several floors of an office environment, a staging area can be set up that includes phones, data lines, desks, and room for files and other business necessities. Then, the first group relocates to this part of the facility while their area is remodeled. Often, departments will be relocated to other floors or another area of the building complicating the phasing process.

7 Gold Standards of Facility Construction

The most important point regarding interior phasing schedules is that the owner, architect and the general contractor must work together as a team to develop the schedule. The owner knows their operation and has the "corporate priority knowledge" that can help guide what needs to be done first. The architect knows the design and the infrastructure of the building, such as mechanical, and electrical systems, and can help guide the process. The GOLD Standard Facilities Contractor, who is responsible for the schedule, provides the following input:

- How long it takes to do the work,

- What material will have to be delivered and removed from the building,

- What needs to be demolished, and how that will impact the infrastructure,

- How to separate the work environment from the construction,

- What needs to be done first from a construction priority,

- What the sequence of sub-contractors will be,

- What the delivery times are for special material, and

- What safety issues exist?

The architect, owner/facility manager and the GOLD Standard Facility Manager working together can develop an interior phasing schedule that is responsive to the owner's needs. As a pre-construction activity, developing the interior phasing schedule can be reflected in the cost, so there are no surprises during construction. Another advantage of the interior phasing schedule is that it helps the employees deal with change, for as long as they know where they are being reallocated to and what the schedule is, they too can plan accordingly.

Construction scheduling requires a team approach. To coordinate, there must be a way to communicate a relatively complex series of events to people who have a construction background, and to some that don't. The schedule is the focal point of that communication process.

Projects change, and a schedule can point out and help identify the impact of those changes on timing, which in turn can affect the business need. A construction schedule helps communicate and set expectations for users of a space who might not otherwise understand why the duration needs to be so long, or why they have to vacate their space to move into another. A construction schedule is a valuable tool used to help communicate the construction process.

George Gogola, CFM from the College of American Pathologists, emphasized three important points regarding construction scheduling. His comments are directed toward the internal perception of a project, and how a construction schedule can help set a tone for a project.

- Scheduling prevents the different contractors on a project from stepping on each other's job.

- Scheduling conveys and enhances the feeling that the project is under control.

- Scheduling minimizes the feeling of chaos.

It's clear that scheduling plays an important role for facility managers regarding projecting project continuity, as this leads to increased productivity, and that's what scheduling in the occupied environment is all about.

3. Fast-Tracking — Fast-tracking allows for an accelerated schedule. Therefore, occupancy will be sooner, and this can be critical. Consider the situation where a facility manager needs a build-out of a space before the Holiday Season. Opening the doors may mean the difference between a profit or a loss.

4. Project Estimates — Project estimates are critical to the success of a project, large or small. It's the estimate that the owner relies upon for funding. The team working together often see ways to reduce the estimate through fast-tracking and developing a responsive schedule.

5. Cost Control — An important aspect of construction management and scheduling is cost control. The actual cost controls are the decisions the Facility Contractor makes as they observe the project. There are many sophisticated construction cost control systems and they are a necessary component that is often overlooked by many contractors.

6. Submittal — The submittal process is an integral part of the construction of a building, affecting everyone on the construction team. The process is initiated by the general contractor as a method of managing the selection of materials, shop drawings, catalog cuts, samples, material mock-ups, test reports, and certificates of compliance. Following is a list of the important points regarding the submittal process.

a. The consensus of expectations is a critical part of the submittal process. At the beginning of the project, the general contractor will outline and discuss with the team what is expected during the submittal process. The goal is to build consensus so that everyone agrees on what to expect. The agreement is necessary because different projects have different scopes of work, which translates into different submittal needs. An example might be to agree on the number of the various samples of glazing that will be used to make the final selection based on the contractor's review of the specifications, availability from the supplier, and other conditions.

b. The submittal log is how the general contractor manages the submittal process. It includes submission dates, required return dates, review by the architect, required delivery of material, and other items relative to the project schedule. Long lead time items receive special consideration as they can impact a project schedule and create tremendous problems in coordination. Shop drawings are also critical to include in the log, as they are used to manufacture or assemble many of the components of the project. A good example of this is steel framing, which must be coordinated down to the last bolt.

c. Response time is equally important as the whole project depends upon what happens next. For example, you can't paint until the colors have been selected, or until the drywall has been installed and taped. The drywall can't go up until the partitions are in place, and rough electrical has been installed. Approval of response time, as developed and managed by the submittal process, become time-critical components to managing the construction schedule.

d. The Jobsite is the final destination of the approved shop drawings, catalog cuts, and approved samples. Here they are used to verify all material shipped to the site. Glazing offers a good example, in which the actual glazing material is compared to the approved glazing sample that was provided by the subcontractor/supplier, approved by the architect, and used as a basis for placing the order. If there is a discrepancy, the general contractor can easily refer to the submittal log to determine the dates of the various approvals, and what criteria were used to place the order. In the end, the submittal log becomes a tool for verification.

Without question, the submittal process, controlled by the submittal log, is a valuable tool for everyone. It's a tool that keeps the project on track, and can help identify long lead issues so the team can respond promptly.

C. CAPITAL EXPENDITURES BUDGET — FOUR-YEAR FACILITY PLAN

A Four-Year Facility Plan is a projection of the facilities major components regarding their projected life due to wear and tear, as well as maintenance. Sometimes referred to as Asset Management, it's basically a four-year spreadsheet listing all of the major elements of the building, including the roof, building envelope, landscaping and paving, HVAC and interior finishes.

The Time Value of Money and Inflation is an important consideration. Something that needs fixing now may cost more in the future.

The goal is to determine what needs attention based on the owner's budget. Do you repair a roof leak, or replace the roof? Should the leaking windows be replaced or new ones installed? The list is endless.

A GOLD Standard Facility Contractor considers the Capital Expenditures Budget and the Four-Year Facility Plan as one of their most important pre-construction services. And since they are truly interested in Cost, Time and Quality, there is no charge for this service. It is simply good planning.

Pre-Construction Services

The GOLD Standard Facility Contractor understands that the only time you can save money on a construction project is before it starts by providing pre-construction services as well as the X-Year Facility Plan. Using these planning tools allows them to see the big picture and take the necessary planning steps to ensure that the project is completed properly.

Chapter Four
Working in the Occupied Environment

WORKING IN THE OCCUPIED ENVIRONMENT can only be done by a skilled and experienced GOLD Standard Facility Contractor to ensure that every detail and possibility is considered. It's an important point for owners to examine and to understand, but unfortunately, many contractors try to dodge the bullet.

Working in the Occupied Environment requires attention to several important concepts that differentiate GOLD Standard Facility Contractors:

A. Staging the Project

B. Site Conditions

C. Three Second Rule

D. Aesthetic Value of Employees

Most people who see an occupied environment project in progress don't realize that this type of work requires an immense amount of experience and planning to make a seamless work day for that company's employees and customers.

As an example, an athletic club started a major remodel of their facility which included demolition, new electrical wiring, lighting, a complete makeover of two large exercise rooms, including wall coverings, flooring, and new video screen. The large, two-story facility, with an indoor running track was open 24 hours a day. The contractor convinced the owner to do the remodel during the day when the facility was fully packed with customers exercising. This meant workmen were walking through the areas while people were exercising carrying 20-foot conduit, electrical wiring, tools, and drywall, etc. They also used the track as a path to where they were working, so it was constantly dirty or closed down. Supplies and building materials should have been brought in at night when the facility was much less occupied. The workers did not wear company shirts, and parked as close to the front of the facility as possible. Instead, there should have been a designated parking area in the back of the facility for them to park. They also made female patrons feel very uncomfortable while they were exercising to have the workers walking through the facility.

They could have easily done this project at night as the facility was open 24 hours a day. They could have staged the working areas better and required their employees to wear company clothing. Occupied environment construction is all about staging; it's all about the customer and the customer's clients.

A. STAGING THE PROJECT

To emphasize the point even further, consider the following Memo from a facility owner:

MEMO
From a Commercial Business

To: Staff
From: The Boss

Re: Work as Usual

Next week is one of the busiest of the year, and we have a lot of projects and contracts to close. In fact, we have daily appointments with clients and prospects. They are flying in from New York, Dallas, and Los Angeles to meet with us. I'll need everyone's cooperation and hard work to accomplish our goals.

Also, the facility is going to be under construction with the East wall coming down, concrete being poured, and a new mechanical system being installed. (Bring a sweater). Good luck and be careful. Arrive early so you can get a parking space before the contractors get them.

The Boss

OK, so the aforementioned memo is somewhat of an exaggeration (I hope), but you probably get the point that this is NOT what working in the occupied environment is all about. Following are some ideas to consider as to what steps a GOLD Standard Facility Contractor takes to expand and monitor safety when working in the occupied environment.

The types of situations referenced in the memo above, however, might happen if the facilities contractor is not experienced in the subtleties of working in occupied environments.

During staging, we also plan how the construction workers get in and out of the facility, and we make sure that they are not the same entrances/exits used by the employees and customers.

In occupied environment construction, a project must be staged, meaning, that what is to be accomplished is compared to what activities are going on in the owner's business. Very often this means doing some of the work in the early morning hours. Or after hours. It also might mean that an area is closed down, or draped in a manner not allowing people inside so that work can be separated from the regular heartbeat of the building.

"In my experience working with a GOLD Standard Facility Contractor, what I enjoy the most is having a mutual understanding of the concept of partnership and a clear vision of what it takes for the Facilities Contractor to work together with the Owner's representative in order to achieve excellent results – especially when your construction site is in the middle of a fully functioning 24/7 facility. All of the minute details need to be taken into consideration, including material delivery routes, staging areas, safety, odor, noise and dust, etc. A GOLD Standard Facility Contractor fully understands that business interruption is not an option when construction work is performed in an occupied environment, and they implement all of the needed procedures in order to avoid it."

Boris Barats, FMP, Affiliate AIA C — Senior Manager, Projects at JLL

B. SITE CONDITIONS

There are four conditions that are of primary importance with close proximity work. They are safety, odor, noise, and dust. Careful planning can control all of these circumstances. The facility manager can and should work closely with their general contractor to reduce inconveniences and disruptions to a normal office routine.

Safety is so important that it's discussed in the following Chapter.

Odor is often one of the most common problems associated with construction and renovation. Ventilation of the construction site may be connected to occupied areas of the building. Also, many mechanical systems are not designed to handle construction odors stemming from paint and other building materials. Painting as much as possible off-site, or in a controlled area, can help minimize this problem. Scheduling construction after peak work hours in well-ventilated areas is another good option. Barricades and rerouting in-office traffic patterns might also be helpful, but is dependent upon the nature of the rehab work being done.

Noise is another problem in an office environment that must be addressed. Again, the use of barricades to seal off the work area can help minimize the noise. Moving materials in and out of the building should be restricted to non-peak work hours. Music should not be played, and loud two-way radios should not be used as sound can carry and amplify within the open space of a construction site devoid of furniture and other materials that dampen sound. Noisy operations, such as nailing in floor plates or core drilling, should be scheduled for non-peak hours or with the use of swing shifts.

Dust is always present in construction and worsens with interior projects where it's captured in a closed environment. Dust can be minimized by setting up a controlled area for the bulk of the cutting work. This area should be well ventilated, and cleaned and wiped down daily, so dust is not tracked through the building. The control area also helps reduce noise.

C. THREE SECOND-RULE

The employees of a GOLD Standard Facility Contractor follow the three-second rule. Very few contractors or sub-contractors follow this rule. It's very simple; it acknowledges the courtesy of all female employees. Historically, everyone has seen or heard of the construction workers who watch women walking down the street and make rude remarks, etc.

A GOLD Standard Facility Contractor's employees are required to avert their eyes within three seconds if they should glance up and see a woman employee. It's a courtesy to the employees and makes it easier for the occupied environment concept to work.

D. AESTHETIC VALUE OF EMPLOYEES

It makes sense also that the employees dress properly. Again, the stereotypical construction worker comes into play as being dressed in dirty clothes, chewing tobacco or with a cigarette hanging out of their mouth. GOLD Standard employees wear a clean uniform with a logo that identifies their company.

The goal is for the construction worker to fit into their work environment. It makes it easier for everyone, and particularly those businesses that depend on customers to come in and make purchases.

Working in the Occupied Environment

Occupied Environment construction means one thing — attention to details. It's what a GOLD Standard Facility Contractor is all about. What might not bother you may be just the one thing that destroys the relationship of your client's customers and their business. Occupied environment construction is necessary because time is money, and if you can help your client keep the doors open, then as a contractor, you've helped them save money.

Chapter Five
Safety Plans For Occupants

SAFETY ALWAYS NEEDS TO BE A PRIMARY FOCUS. The safety of both on-site construction workers and the employees and guests at the building must be protected. Construction has inherent hazards that cannot be ignored. Even when a building system fails, safety and response time is all important.

A. CONSTRUCTION AND SAFETY

To ensure safety, whether it's an occupied environmental project or a new ground-up building, all areas under construction must be secured to keep non-essential personnel, or curious employees, from intentionally or unintentionally entering the construction site. Barricades, signage, and strict enforcement are the best ways to avoid safety issues. Insurance is mandatory to cover the site's employees, and others, often with additional insurance provisions or blanket policies.

A GOLD Standard Facility Contractors contractor experienced in the occupied environment will take the necessary steps to make sure that safety is addressed. A veteran contractor knows how to staff the project with the right crew. The skilled workers must be aware of their environment, and adhere to all safety regulations. Also, they must be professional in their appearance, (no torn jeans), etc. and be courteous and always be mindful of their manners and language. Workers should never wander into, visit, or congregate in areas within the building outside the scope of the construction, cafeteria, and washrooms. Essentially, the construction crew workers must be able to operate within an occupied environment. Working in occupied spaces is a specialty that requires a contractor who has experience.

B. CONTRACTOR SAFETY PLANS

Safety is an integral part of the construction process. It's probably the single most important issue every diligent contractor faces. For example, an owner who needs to remodel and/or add-on to an existing facility cannot afford to relocate the entire office to a temporary facility; financially, this is not feasible. The solution is for the owner or the facility manager to seek out a facility contractor who is an expert in working in the occupied environment. The owner bears the responsibility of making sure their employees and visitors to the facility are safe during the construction process.

However, working in the occupied environment creates additional safety concerns from both the owner's and the contractor's perspective. There must be two safety plans; a safety plan for the construction work environment, and a saftey plan for the all the employees and customers using the facility.

From the contractor perspective, safety is an on-going everyday issue. There are many OSHA regulations that a contractor must follow that provide guidelines for safety. The contractor is also faced with worker's compensation insurance based on industry standards. As a consequence, the contractor has a regular program for educating their workers regarding safety issues. There is a strong commitment to safety from top management all the way down to the job site.

It's the job site where the owner and the contractor meet. When there is going to be construction in an occupied environment, there are important steps that can be initiated that directly relate to safety. Temporary staging areas can be set up, work can occur before and after office hours, and the movement of traffic patterns for people and materials can be managed. The owner relies on the contractor for their expertise of construction safety issues.

There are two important factors an owner/facility manager can evaluate to determine the safety qualifications of a contractor. They are as follows:

The Insurance Experience Modification Rate, (EMR), is an industry standard. It's an experience-rating factor that judges all contractors in specific categories. An EMR rate higher than 1.00 means that the contractor's premiums will be higher than that of an average company in the same category. For example, a rating of 1.10 means the contractor will pay a 10% surcharge on insurance. A rating of .90 means the contractor will have earned a 10% credit on their base workers compensation premiums.

An owner/facility manager reviewing several contractors can ask for their modification rate as part of their proposal, and quickly determine by an industry standard the safety history of the contractor.

The Contractor's Safety Program is also an important yardstick for judging a contractor's commitment to safety. There are several key questions that can be asked that provide background regarding safety:

- What are the safety programs a contractor has established?

- Is there a full-time safety manager?

- Are there Toolbox Seminars, or on-site safety presentations on a regular basis?

- What kinds of testing do the employees receive on an annual basis relative to safety?

- What kinds of training programs are the employees required to attend?

- Does the contractor have safety manuals?

Safety starts with planning during pre-construction activities, and it never stops until the end of the project. Such considerations as how the site is laid out, and where the materials are stored, are important. Often, safety gets overlooked when many different activities are going on at the same time; this is particularly important when there is a lot of on-site labor with various trades working together. A clean site is critical to safety as well as the maintenance of tools and construction equipment.

Drug and alcohol testing is also part of the safety program as it becomes a red flag for accidents waiting to happen, because of worker impairment. Special considerations for confined space entry, heavy equipment safety, and hazardous materials are also important issues that need to be considered. Safety is important, and it's everyone's concern and responsibility.

C. DISASTER RECOVERY PLANS

Sometimes bad things happen to good buildings, such as a fire or flood. Facility Managers have been able to make a direct comparison to the response time and the cost of the repair and clean-up and repair efforts. The faster the designated team can get on site, the lower the cost. Consider this example: let's say a small community town is relatively large and growing. The growth is on the west side of the town where there is vacant land. What if there was only one fire department located on the east side of town, and a fire breaks out. You must wait until the fire department arrives, and meanwhile, your building burns. Now, what if a second fire station had been built, say next door to your property? There would be no wait.

Considering the two scenarios which is going to cost you more money? Of course, you know the answer. Even though this example is dramatized to make a point, it demonstrates clearly that response time is critical when something happens to a building. That is why having a Disaster Recovery Plan (DRP) in place is a must for all buildings.

Now, following is another example of NOT having a Disaster Recovery Plan, compared to what would happen if a company DID HAVE a Disaster Recovery Plan in-place.

Example: A Burst Water Pipe in a Multiple Story Building

A Restoration contractor responds to a high rise building where a water supply pipe burst above a drop down ceiling in a cubical area of health care provider-tenant. The source of the leak is a domestic water supply line that feeds the restrooms on the 6th floor. The Restoration Team is contacted and sends out three trucks with two technicians in each truck to address the water intrusion. It is reported to have begun to show itself on the floors below.

The technicians show up at the same time and are circling the parking lot looking for a parking spot and/or the loading dock. They are calling the property manager multiple times, but nobody is answering the phone, and they can't find a place to park. They get a call back from the engineer after 30 min of being on site telling them how to get to the loading dock which is located on the West side of the building and is accessed by a ramp leading down to the loading dock (time wasted 3 man hours). The techs drive around and get to the loading dock where they are met by the building engineer and are taken up to the floors above.

The technicians bring their extraction equipment and begin the extraction process while the supervisor inspects the property for damage. The supervisor is in need of floor plans to create a moisture map for documentation purposes and also as required by the insurance company. He has asked the building engineer if he has those and the building engineer acknowledged that they did but he had no idea where they were at and had no time to look for them due to the emergency.

The supervisor is now required to measure and draw the entire affected area as well as surrounding areas by hand on paper (time wasted 3 man hours during the initial call). The supervisor is not able to complete the map accurately and missed a couple rooms because with all the commotion he was asked to participate in conversations with property management and the tenants. This is not discovered until later on in the day and required a follow-up visit to correct the mistake (time wasted 2 man hours for drive time and on-site time).

After the extraction was completed and the crew discovered that there was a small closet located on the 4th floor that had boxes of files stored in it. The closet was locked, and only the office manager had the key. The initial crew did not realize it was affected due to the door being shut and they assumed that the water did not make it to the 4th floor since the surrounding areas were dry.

What Would Have Happened if They had a Disaster Recovery Plan in Place?

If the DRP were in place, the restoration contractor would have been able to save time and money for the client. When the crew was circling the building, they were wasting precious time and burning man hours that were ultimately billed to the client. Time wasted was 8 man hours @ $45.00 per hour equals $360.00.

In addition to that, the supervisor missed a wet area because he was lost in the layout of the building. Having the floor plans ahead of time would have allowed them to see that the tenant build-out placed a storage closet below a break room and thus it had concrete floor penetrations for the plumbing. Knowing this is very crucial when detecting moisture and preventing additional damages.

The files that were located in that room were irreplaceable, and could have been saved if the supervisor had known that it is absolutely necessary to inspect the surrounding affected areas. His judgment call was based on the conditions present on that floor and not the knowledge of the entire building. This is very common when sending techs out who do not have all the information available to them.

One can conclude that a Disaster Recovery Plan in-place and constantly updated is an important part of Facility Management. That's the difference between a facility companies that do not offer GOLD Standard of Facility Construction Services.

D. SAFETY PLAN FOR THE BUILDING'S USERS

Just like the construction workers, the employees who use the building must also have a safety plan. The employees use the facility, but there may also be customers who access the facility, such as a bank, a clothing store in a mall, or even a restaurant.

The priority is the safe passage of the users on the site and not being able to unintentionally walk into an area of construction. A safe passage gets more complicated when elevators are involved. Everything must be planned for, such as moving equipment and material and supplies in the evening hours to the cleaning crews that make sure the building is presentable in the morning.

In cases where a strip shopping mall is being remodeled, all of the tenants must be continually updated on the construction activity schedule, as parking needs may shift. Blocking the passage of customers is not acceptable, so signage becomes important.

There is another plan that is important, and that's the Facility Emergency Plan. Every commercial building should have one of these plans, but one should exist especially when there is a remodel going on.

E. FACILITY EMERGENCY PLAN

Here's the problem: You get a call in the middle of the night, and the cleaning service has found water dripping from a lower floor ceiling in your facility. The problem gets worse. Upon inspection, it was realized that it was from sprinkler pipes located two floors above. The water is coming down a partition wall and eventually soaking several computer terminals. There are plumbing, drywall, painting and electrical problems to deal with, but the problem still gets worse. It's your busiest part of the month, and there's no way to shut down or move the operation. Work must continue. Now, what do you do? The cleaning staff is telling you to get someone down there to fix it. The place is a mess, and they can't clean it until the problem is solved.

The management of a facility includes what happens when there is an emergency problem. Problems can be a banging door in a storm, a leaking pipe, or a full-blown disaster. In any case, you must be prepared because little problems can sometimes turn into big problems if not dealt with right away. Often the solution requires multiple trades, all of which must be coordinated. If a Facility Emergency Plan is not in place, your alternative is to start with the yellow pages and try to find different vendors that you need, but there is a risk of getting someone that you are unfamiliar with who has no expertise. This is not the time to be pursuing references. If you do have a Facility Emergency Plan in place, that includes a general contractor who has all the contacts with the different trades, vendors, and suppliers you may need, then the solution to the problem is one phone call away.

> "When working with a GOLD Standard Facility Contractor, I know I will get integrity, expertise, consistency and the high quality work that I expect. It is refreshing not to have to micro manage my GC for our tenant improvement projects in the future."
>
> TOM CRUZ, CFM, OSS

To get started, or to review your current plan, you might ask these three questions:

- Does your company have a Facility Emergency Plan in place?

- Have procedures been established to protect essential records including computer files?

- Do you have a relationship with an outside vendor as part of your plan?

- Do you have a Disaster Recovery Plan that is updated on a regular basis?

As you review these questions, also consider the following key steps you can implement that will help manage emergencies:

- Develop a Facility Emergency Plan that has specific goals and objectives to handle emergencies and/or true disasters.

- Set up a team of subcontractors, vendors, and suppliers all tied to a Single Source of Responsibility that can provide coordination and supervision of the different building.

- Ensure there is a 24-hour access number to that Single Source of Responsibility.

- Test your team. Know the response time and where you might have a weakness that needs attention.

- Make sure safety is part of the disaster recovery program.

- Verify that all members of the team have the appropriate insurance to work at your facility, and have supporting documents on file.

- Make sure you or your Single Source of Responsibility has access to rental equipment, which can become scarce in true emergency situations.

In an actual disaster, the demand for general contractors increases dramatically, and having them as part of your team may provide additional resources. With a good relationship in place, the answer to the question of the burst water pipe is to contact your Single Source of Responsibility provider. That kicks off a series of events that takes care of the problem by someone you know, who knows your facility, and has a qualified team of subcontractors, vendors, and suppliers in place that are ready to work in your facility.

The amount of money saved due to damage such as a burst water pipe, a leaking roof, or other unseen events could be significant. You can't afford NOT to have a plan in place.

F. SITE SAFETY

A construction company must coordinate and team up with subcontractors that can gear their operation to fit the project schedule. The general contractor and subcontractors must be able to move construction workers from one project site to another.

In both retail and commercial job sites, it is critical to work within the given pedestrian and vehicular traffic flow restrictions. Movement of materials into and out of a building must be done at times that do not impact the lobbies, elevators, and hallways. Parking and traffic lanes must not be blocked during peak hours of use.

- **Added Security** — Early morning and late afternoon-evening shifts might require the addition of security to a facility. While it may add a small cost of the project, it serves to protect both the owner and the contractor from unexpected situations and allows work to occur when people are not normally at the facility.

- **Clean-up** — The site must be cleaned up after each day's work. Particularly in interior work, dust must be avoided. All occupied areas adjacent to the work areas must be cleaned so that it does not interfere with the client's work. A clean site, with materials stored properly, also contributes to a more efficient operation.

7 Gold Standards of Facility Construction

A stealth construction operation means the contractor is responding to the needs of the owner. It means that a team of players working together can provide construction services that do not needlessly impact the existing operation of a retail or commercial facility. The GOLD standard Facility Contractor can respond to the need, coordinate the necessary sub to save the owner money and together, a construction project is completed that makes everyone proud.

Safety Plans For Occupants

GOLD STANDARD

Safety. Safety and Safety. For everyone. That's the goal, and nothing less than that is acceptable.

Chapter Six
Information Transfer

AT THE END OF THE PROJECT there are always tasks to be completed. Unfortunately, this is where many contractors fail to follow through on a timely manner. For example, it's quite common for some projects to have an open punch list for several weeks after the project has been completed. There are several reasons for this, but the most common reason is that the contractor is on to another project where they are able to create more cash flow. Whatever the reason, here are several ideas to consider when your project is in this stage.

WHAT HAPPENS AND WHEN IT HAPPENS

First, make sure you include the right people in the closeout process. For example, during the building walk-through that includes the HVAC system, the building engineer or the person responsible for that equipment must be present.

Second, consider using a building project as a catalyst to organize your own internal information. More and more companies are moving toward the use of software that is a facility-based information system. In other words, all necessary information can be accessed through software to manage the facility and its components.

Third, since many of the certification procedures can be complicated and include a lot of technical detail, work with the contractor to videotape these segments, so you have an exact record of the instructions regarding specific equipment. These recordings will also be very valuable when training new employees.

It's part of the contractor's contractual responsibility to initiate the closeout process; to gather all the pertinent information, and to schedule the various meetings. This transfer of information requires diligent attention to details, which ultimately will help the operation of the building.

A. PROJECT CLOSEOUT

A project closeout is initiated by the general contractor following guidelines set-up by the architect. This process ensures that all necessary information about the building and its components, including how the project was built, are transferred to the owner or the owner's representative.

The closeout process includes the following transfer of information:

- **Operational and Maintenance Manuals** — Includes all functioning building components and specifications and selections of all finish materials.

- **As-Built Drawings** — A record of all concealed work for future reference.

- **Permit Cards** — Documents that are fully executed by building inspection officials.

- **Warranties and Guarantees** — Documents standard one-year warranties and special guarantee periods.

- **Final Walk-Through** — A walk-through of the facility noting conditions and items for the punch list, as well as answering questions from the owner.

- **Punch List** — A list of items prepared by the project manager that is to be completed.

- **Technology Certification** — Special training on technical equipment.

- **Digital Technologies and Transfers** — Transfer to the owner.

- **Contract Closeout** — Notice of completion and final payment.

- **One-Year Walk-Through** — A follow-up process in which the owner and contractor review the building relative to general and special warranties.

The above list is not an exclusive, but merely an indication as to the scope that the project closeout procedure entails.

The closeout process gathers all the important information about the project, from the HVAC system to the type of carpet used in the facility.

For example, the operational and maintenance manuals will detail exactly how the carpet should be maintained in terms of cleaning supplies, materials, frequency, etc., and if there is a problem what future steps should be taken to correct it.

B. A REAL PUNCH LIST SOLUTION

The punch list is one of the most important tools in closing out a job. However, punch lists often get a bad rap. Some project managers feel that if the general contractor were doing their job, there would be no need for a punch list. Others feel that some general contractors push too many items to the punch list, so they can come back and finish the work later while allowing their workers to move on to another project. As a result, the punch list becomes a nagging source of aggravation for both the facility manager and the general contractor.

The worst case scenario is when a punch list is identified, and the contractor does not finish the list in a timely manner, or not at all. Granted, there can be extenuating circumstances, such as back ordered products or equipment damaged during shipping, etc. but, for the most part, the punch list should be completed in a relatively short period and good communication between the facility manager and the contractor should remain ongoing.

> "In my opinion, the two most valuable components that can be lost during a project are time and money, once they are gone you cannot get them back and the net effect of losing both results in changing the future of other projects both planned and unplanned at the time of completion. In the facilities management world, project management can effect a whole lot more than just time and money, it directly effects employee productivity, comfort and safety, just to name a few. A GOLD Standard Facility Contractor understands this issue of time and money, and that's what sets them apart from anyone in our market. Their overall awareness of what project management really encompasses to ensure an effective and efficient project, time and time again is a critical part of the project."
>
> BEAU HARTWELL, CFM

The reality of the situation is there will always be some pending punch list items to complete. The nature of construction is that it brings together many different materials, combined with many different types of workers, creating situations in which a few corrections may be necessary. When the final punch list is compiled, it's an opportunity to view the project through different sets of eyes. It's also an opportunity to demonstrate that no detail is too small or too large.

Without going into an in-depth analysis of punch lists, the following guidelines should provide a basis for both the facility manager and the general contractor regarding mutual expectations.

- **Pre-punch list inspection:** As work is completed, each portion of the work should receive a pre-punch list review by the general contractor before the project closeout and final punch list. This really helps in the overall process as it helps to ensure that work is completely finished before the project teams leave, thereby greatly minimizing the final punch list items.

- **The final occupancy date:** The final occupancy date should always be kept in mind as the project proceeds, and the issues that must be corrected for occupancy purposes should be focused upon to minimize any occupancy problems and inconvenience to the building manager.

- **No scope changes:** The punch list is one of the final elements for project completion and is not a time for scope changes. If the scope changes, then this must be addressed as a separate issue from the main punch list.

- **Technology:** Punch lists should be generated using integrated construction project management software. This will ensure all the punch list items are captured that is customized for that project. The punch list can also be sorted a number of different ways, with places for signatures by the various trades when an item is completed.

- **Teamwork:** Include members of the various trades on the final punch list inspection, as this improves the communication process and gives the trades, whose work may affect each other, a chance to figure out the best way to correct a particular problem.

The punch list is an important part of the facility manager's responsibility and one in which the contractor can help. Without question, the punch list allows the general contractor to demonstrate they are part of the facility manager's team, and they will do anything to help everyone feel comfortable on the day of occupancy. Doing so reflects the contractor's commitment to their client. The punch list is more than a list of things to do – *it's an opportunity to exceed expectations.*

C. ONE YEAR FOLLOW-UP AND WARRANTY

The one-year follow-up is critical from the owners' point-of-view. The reason is there are warranties in place. In order to exercise any warranty options, the different components should be inspected. Many contractors skip this important step.

However, a GOLD Standard Facility Contractor will schedule a meeting, with the building maintenance staff or the building engineer, to walk through the entire project including every level, including the roof. The components such as mechanical, electrical, roofing systems, etc., are all observed, and notations made as to their condition and if there is any action needed.

This is a key step and an important one.

Information Transfer

GOLD STANDARD

A building consists of many complex components all designed to work together to provide a harmonious environment with the aesthetics that complement the activities on the inside as well as letting light in, while responding to the environment as suggested by the LEED programs. With that said, the hand-off from the contractor to the owner is a critical step so that they become familiar with the different components. Likewise, warranty issues must be addressed within the proper time frame. A good contractor is going to be there to answer questions and to assist in any way possible.

Chapter Seven
A New Way To Manage

THE BEGINNING OF THIS BOOK was about contractor selection. Several ideas were presented to assist an owner or a facility manager in selecting a GOLD Standard Facility Contractor. The selection process includes how construction services are delivered, the differences between a broker contractor and one that self-performs the work, the importance of having a superintendent or a working foreperson on the job site at all times, as well as the concept that the low bidder is not always the best.

However, there is one more important aspect to consider, and that is how the contractor and the owner think regarding their working relationship, and how services are provided.

Consider the following scenario: A facility manager of several commercial properties bids out all the projects on a competitive basis as a way to get the best price. After a couple of years, he notices a trend that one contractor who specializes in facility work is always in the running for the project. On top of that, the facility contractor has several value-added services that make them very competitive and attractive to the facility manager. One day the owner/facility manager has a major emergency in one of the facilities. With no time to develop the necessary bidding documents, he calls up the facility contractor that had demonstrated a fair and best price.

> "My interactions with a GOLD Standard Facility Contractor have demonstrated to me that they place great emphasis on customer service. They understand the value and importance of providing excellent customer service and has instilled it in their employees and subcontractors. A GOLD Standard Facility Contractor ensures that their customers are fully engaged in the development of the scope of work to ensure their needs are incorporated into the proposals. As part of the focus is on customer service, they continuously keep their customers informed of the status of their project."
>
> TED RITTER - LEED AP, CBD, PMP, IFMA Fellow

The facility manager and the facility contractor discuss the situation, and the contractor asks several questions and identifies several areas the facility manager had missed. After talking, they decide to partner on the project. Since some of the work can start immediately, the project saves money right up front as the rest of the project takes shape. The partnering is a success, and the facility manager decides to start using the facility contractor on a regular basis.

A. PARTNERING

A GOLD Standard Facilities Contractor will often partner on many projects as there are so many benefits for all involved. This scenario is also referred to as being their client's in-house construction department. They want to be the company that not only focuses on the project, but also envisions about the long-range planning of the facility regarding capital expenditures, and be able to provide their value-added services.

Partnering is a method of delivering construction services whereby the owner and a GOLD Standard Facility Contractor team up to do a project or a series of projects together. This process delivers projects on a cost-effective and timely basis because it builds upon a philosophy of trust, respect, and long-term relationships. There are many variations of partnering, and many ways it can be initiated as a project management process. But partnering works best when an owner and a facility contractor develop a relationship to the point that a team is built early in the life of a project. A strategic alliance is built whereby the contractor takes the lead role in the project management and essentially quarterbacks the decision-making process.

There are many advantages for the owner and the facility manager who build this relationship. For example, an owner who has developed a partnering relationship can rely on the contractor they partner with, and have immediate access to construction specialist at any time day or night. Whether it's to fix a lock on a door, or repair a damaged roof that threatens merchandise or the contents of a warehouse; the contractor can take care of the problem. Because the relationship is built upon past experience and mutual trust and cooperation, there are no questions as to billing, contracts or change orders being signed before doing the work. *The owner and the contractor are on the same team.* The contractor is an extension of that company; they are essentially an outsourced construction department.

The partnering process has another advantage in that an owner or an owner's representative can bring them in during the preliminary planning stages of a project. Those who are going to deliver the finished project can answer questions and provide input as the project develops. Now, such things as project schedules, winter conditions, working in an occupied environment, can be answered immediately and without any delays. Partnering develops a team whereby decisions are reached faster within a framework of cooperation.

GOLD Standard Facility partnering also works from the point-of-view of the architect. There are obviously a lot of advantages to partnering, some of which are mentioned below:

- The team knows and works well with each other,

- There is an agreed upon method to solve problems,

- Decision-making is expedited,

- Increased construction innovation and creativity,

- The team can count on each other to be there when there is a problem,

- Reduced administration expense,

- Easier coordination of safety issues,

- Fast-tracking is easier, and

- The owner saves money.

Compared to the traditional method of "Bid-and-Build," where the contractor's input comes in last, the partnering method of delivering construction services offers many advantages to owners and to those who regularly manage facilities. Why wait until the end to get input from those who are going to be responsible for building the project? Buildings are complicated, the building process is complex; partnering makes it easier for everyone.

As indicated, there are many variations to the partnering process. Sometimes the process starts before drawings are generated, and at other times it starts before bidding. An owner working with their architect may team-up on bid submissions. Hence, team presentations are made so the owner and architect can judge all of the players for each of the different bids. Or, a team may be partnered together to make a bid as a marketing tool when team presentations are not required to stand out from the rest of the bidders. In this case, they are saying:

We are the best team for this project. We can save you money because we have joined resources.

Another advantage of partnering is a team attracts itself to multiple projects. Some owners do multiple projects that may or may not be repetitious. It may be retail stores, facility build-outs, remodeling, or corporate work. The prudent owner may decide to develop a permanent team of players who partner with each other on all of the owner's projects.

The teamwork extends down through the contractor's organization. As the contractor is the quarterback of construction, they can also develop partnering relationships with various key subcontractors. These key subcontractors will make themselves and their crews available for immediate response when an owner or a general contractor have a need.

- Partnering is an entirely different mindset.

- There are no surprises.

- You'll have confidence in what is going on at your facility.

- You control the costs.

- You can plan ahead, and there are no charges.

- You can exceed expectations.

Once it's determined that the facility contractor's price is competitive, a team relationship can be built that can save an owner money. At this point the facility contractor works with you and not for you. There are all kinds of advantages, one being is they carry all of the insurance for anything going on in your facility, and they will provide free value engineering regarding the long-range planning. It's an OPEN BOOK / COST PLUS relationship where the owner knows exactly where all the money is being spent. There is no markup of any sub-trade or materials.

A New Way To Manage

GOLD STANDARD

Using the partnering facilities delivery method provides multiple benefits to the owner including there are no hidden costs because of the OPEN BOOK/COST PLUS services. This is the very best way to take care of your facility and save money in the process. Everyone agrees that the facility contractor should be paid fairly, and once this is determined, now you can direct the work that needs to be done and take advantage of all the Value-Added Services that a GOLD Standard Facility Contractor provides. The reason that other delivery services are so tumultuous is that fees are hidden, and everyone is trying to get their share. GOLD Standard Facility Contractor's approach to In-House Construction Services eliminates these problems. It's the best-kept secret around.

Conclusion
The Gold Standard Facility Contractor

The Real Secret to Facility Construction

FACILITY CONSTRUCTION HAS SEVERAL ABSOLUTES that must exist in order for the client to recieve a clean project. The word "clean" is used to illustrate that construction, as experienced by many, is a battle between the client, the architect, the contractor, and the sub-contractor. The end result is that client ends up paying more money – that's not the way to do business.

As we've stated before, it must be remembered that there are contractors and sub-contractors who bid low, and then use any reason to ask for more money and time via a change order, even though all these questionable areas should be identified during the bidding process. But there might be other reasons. Sometimes a contractor only wants a change order for more time which delays the owner's occupancy. Why? Because, as mentioned before, the contractor may have landed a new project and by getting a delay they can move their workers to get the new contract started.

"Today's construction world is different than it used to be and will continue to evolve into a more process-based industry than ever before; the process is a series of connected events. Yes, there will always be questions. Yes, issues will arise. But when everyone is working together as a team, issues can be addressed and questions can be answered and solutions can be identified that do not jeopardize the quality of the project."

Many GOLD Standard Facility Contractors have embraced systems methodologies as promoted and taught by Dean Kashiwagi, Professor at Arizona State University, which is an outsourcing methodology that organizes and implements the construction sequences to provide the services to build the building.

GOLD Standard Facility Contractors encourage partnering, so they can provide their value-added services and facility planning expertise to the facility manager. Construction should be a team project, not an adversarial nightmare of change orders and delays.

Appendix

Disaster Recovery Plan
Example Documents

BELOW IS A SAMPLE LIST THAT CHARACTERIZES the type of information that needs to be gathered and verified for a Disaster Recovery Plan. There could be more, or less, depending upon the building and the use of that building, as well as location.

Disaster Recovery Plan

Water, Fire, Mold, Biohazard. Asbestos

Table of Contents

1. CONTACT INFORMATION

    A. Contact Information For Restoration Company

2. SERVICE STANDARDS

    A. Who Initiates The Calls?

    B. Who Signs the Work Authorization?
After The Call and The First Responder Has Been Dispatched To The Job, Who Gets Notified?

C. Daily Updates

D. Insurance Activation Protocol

E. Discover Mold, Asbestos, or Pre-Existing Damage

F. Reconstruction/Permanent Repairs Contracts

G. Invoicing Procedures

H. Contracts

3. READINESS PLAN

A. Property Info

1. Property Name:

2. General Manager Name:

3. Address (Full address with City, State & Zip Code)

B. Arrival-First Man In

1. Where does Restoration Company park their vehicles?

2. Where do you prefer the Restoration Company to access the building?

3. Can we access the elevators to move equipment?

4. Do we need to pad the elevators?

5. Do you have required floor protection to move equipment through the lobby?

6. Where is the elevator equipment room?

7. Does the elevator pit have a sump pump?

8. Are you able to access the elevator pit without contacting the elevator vendor?

9. Elevator vendor?

10. Do Restoration Company employees need to sign in and out of the building?

C. Building Information

1. Type of construction:

2. Number of stories:

3. Number of suites:

4. Original construction date:

5. Most recent renovation date:

D. Interior

1. What areas of the building are glued down carpet?

1. Which lobby areas have a pad?

3. What type of pad is installed in the building?

4. Does the building have carpet base cove, rubber or wood?

5. Location of water shut off valves for each level?

E. Electrical

1. Electrical vendor

2. Location of electrical panel room:

3. Location of the main electrical disconnect switch to shut off electricity to the building:

4. Please provide restoration company with the amperage, volt age, and phasing generally posted on the disconnect switch (the disconnect switch is where the entire electrical supply comes into the building and is where all power can be shut off to the building).

5. Is there an emergency generator on the property?

6. If yes, what is it set up to run? (Part of the building, entire building, suite only, etc.)

7. The restoration company has the capability of providing you with an emergency generator should the need arise in a disaster event. If a generator is requested, where would it be parked to allow for easy access to the main electrical disconnect switch and a clear path to run wiring from the generator to the disconnect switch?

8. How many feet from the generator to disconnect switch?

F. Fire Suppression

1. Location of sprinkler valve shut-offs:

2. Do you have a dry fire suppression system in the attic?

3. Fire suppression vendor:

G. Plumbing

1. Plumbing vendor:

H. General

1. HVAC vendor:

2. It vendor:

3. Location of chemical storage:

4. Additional pertinent information:

5. Who would the Restoration Company contact to order replacement FF & E or any brand specific materials that are needed to put the damaged areas back to pre-loss condition?

6. Please also email layout of your property or fire plan layout to above email address. Thank you!

4. SHUT OFF VALVE LOCATIONS

5. EXECUTED DRP AGREEMENT

6. FLOOR PLANS SDS

QUESTIONS THAT GOLD STANDARD FACILITY CONTRACTORS ARE FREQUENTLY ASKED

1. What services does a Gold Standard Facility Contractor provide?

2. As a facility contractor and facility manager, what is your firm's background?

3. I have an emergency project. What do I do?

4. What makes your firm different from other firms we might interview?

5. Do you use any technology that gives you a strategic advantage over your competition?

6. Do you self-perform?

7. Who can I call about your work?

8. If you use subcontractors, how do you qualify them?

9. How do you monitor the cost of a project versus the budget and contract price?

10. How do you manage punch lists?

11. Do you schedule each project?

12. What is your geographic coverage?

13. Can you work with me to reduce costs?

14. Are you available 24 hours a day 7 days a week?

15. How can you identify a GOLD Standard Facility Contractor?

7 Gold Standards of Facility Construction

7 Gold Standards of Facility Construction

Author Bio
Tom Pritscher, LEED® AP, FMP

Tom Pritscher, LEED® AP, FMP is the President and Founder of TEPCON Construction Inc., a full-service general contracting firm based in Tempe, AZ. With more than 4 decades of experience in the industry, he learned his skills as a second-generation commercial contractor at the young age of 14 years old. After earning his construction management degree with honors from Southern Illinois University, Carbondale, Pritscher worked in various areas of the construction industry, including as a Project Manager, VP of Business Development, Executive VP for Tenant Improvement, and much more.

Along with his duties at TEPCON, Pritscher is also the Co-Founder and Principal of DrawAlert, a Construction Administration Software built to provide end-to-end transparency on construction projects. As someone who regularly gives back to his community, Pritscher likes to volunteer his time, knowledge, and talents as a mentor and internship-provider for college students in the IFMA student chapter as well as Arizona State University. Because of his constant advocation for Facilities Management, Pritscher spent more than two decades on IFMA's Board of Directors, and continues to work closely with the organization today.

Pritscher's personal values stand on the pillars of respect, teamwork, and safety. He utilizes these standards outside of his career, as well as bringing a unique cultural shift to the TEPCON team and its focus on projects, facilities, and restoration. From top-to-bottom, Pritscher and his team at TEPCON share the same core values, and ensure that each project embodies these qualities.

Co-Author Bio
Ronald A. McKenzie, NCARB

RONALD A. MCKENZIE is a licensed architect in the State of California, and holds an up-to-date NCARB Record File of his experience. Ron is president of COMPASS Consultants Corporation, a business planning and marketing company that focuses on the construction industry helping to guide their direction and growth. He has worked with Tom Pritscher for over twenty-five years on business development and marketing projects.

Ron's architectural knowledge gives him a unique perspective on the business of architecture, construction, engineering and how construction services are delivered, including facility services. Ron has authored several books on marketing and business development for the construction industry, including *THE KING AND THE MOAT CONTRACTOR, MARKETING CONFIDENTIAL: 101 Secrets to Increase Profits in the Construction Industry, BAROQUE MARKETING: Is your Construction Marketing Broke? FEDERAL FEAR FACTORS, and also HOW TO WIN MORE CONSTRUCTION PROJECTS: 7 Strategic Tactics to Differentiate Your Company at RFP Factors.*

Contact Info

Tom Pritscher, LEED® AP, FMP
TEPCON Construction, Inc.
tom@tepcon.com

with
Ronald A. McKenzie, NCARB
COMPASS Consulting Corporation
ramckenzie.compass@gmail.com